This book
belongs to:

_____

_____

_____

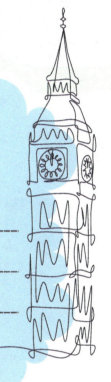

© Copyright 2024 - All rights reserved.

The contents of this book may not be reproduced, duplicated, or transmitted without direct written permission from the author.

Under no circumstances will any legal responsibility or blame be held against the publisher for any reparation, damages, or monetary loss due to the information herein, either directly or indirectly.

Legal Notice:

You cannot amend, distribute, sell, use, quote, or paraphrase any part of the content within this book without the consent of the author.

Disclaimer Notice:

Please note the information contained within this document is for educational and entertainment purposes only. No warranties of any kind are expressed or implied. Readers acknowledge that the author is not engaging in the rendering of legal, financial, medical, or professional advice. Please consult a licensed professional before attempting any techniques outlined in this book.
By reading this document, the reader agrees that under no circumstances is the author responsible for any losses, direct or indirect, which are incurred as a result of the use of the information contained within this document, including, but not limited to, —errors, omissions, or inaccuracies.

Table of Contents

Introduction
- Welcome to Your London Adventure!
- How to Use This Travel Guide
- Before You Arrive in London - Journal Prompts

Part I – Discovering London's Iconic Landmarks
- Buckingham Palace: The King's Royal Residence
- Play 'I Spy the Guard' Game at Buckingham Palace
- Meet Beefeaters & Ravens at The Tower of London
- Crown Jewels Treasure Hunt at the Tower of London
- Seek Out the Secrets of Westminster Abbey
- Speak in Secret at St. Paul's Cathedral
- Get an Eyeful of London on the Millennium Wheel
- Take Time Out at The Palace of Westminster

Part II – Museum Monsters & Mummies
- Old World Adventures & Priceless Treasures Await at The British Museum
- Prehistoric Adventures at the Natural History Museum
- Hands-on Fun for Curious Minds at the Science Museum
- Discover the Wonderful World of Art and Design at the V&A Museum
- Time Travel Through The Streets of London

Part III – Adventuring in London's Enchanting Parks and Palaces
- Hyde Park: London's Green Oasis
- Have a Splashing Summer at Hyde Park
- Pelicans, Playgrounds and Picnics at St. James's Park
- Nature Detective in The Regent's Park
- Pirate Adventures in Peter Pan's Playground at Kensington Gardens
- Medieval Adventures & A Maze Challenge in Haunted Hampton Court

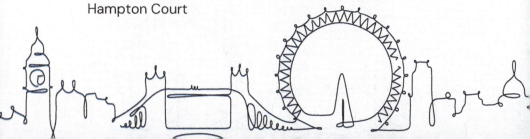

Part IV - Uncovering London's Quirky Attractions

- Crack the Case at the Sherlock Holmes Museum
- Jump Scares & Historical Drama in the London Dungeon
- Only The Bravest Survive the Terrors of The London Dungeon
- Selfies With Stars at Madame Tussauds
- Take an Interactive Tour of London's Oldest and Most Haunted Prison

Part V - Family Feasts on London's Streets

- Traditional British Treats From Fish 'n' Chips to Sherry Trifle
- Street Food Feast at Borough Market
- Take a Tasting Tour of Borough Market With Drinks & Nibbles
- Get a Taste of True British Tradition With Afternoon Tea
- London's Best Kid-Friendly Restaurants
- How to Be a London Foodie

Part VI - Navigating London

- Getting About on the London Tube
- Play The Tube Station Scavenger Hunt
- Riding London's Iconic Red Buses
- Traveling & Tipping in Black Taxis
- River Thames Boat Rides & Bridges
- Play The London Landmark Bingo Game

Part VII - West End Shows & Market Mania

- Dazzling Entertainment Awaits in the West End's Theatreland
- Put on Your Own West End Show
- Quirkiness & Circus Acts at Covent Garden
- Have a Luvly Jubbly Day Out at London's Markets
- Market Mania Scavenger Hunt
- Speak Slang Like a Local Londoner

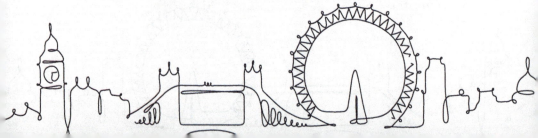

Part VIII – Magical Day Trips Outside London

- Backstage on the Harry Potter Movie Set at Warner Bros. Studio
- Make a Hit Movie Like Harry Potter
- A Royal Day Out at Windsor Castle
- Building Adventures for All Ages at Legoland Windsor Resort
- Become A Master Builder at Legoland

Part IX – London Facts & Trivia

- Have You Got The Knowledge?
- Famous Londoners Who Shaped British Culture & History
- A New London Rises From The Ashes After The Great Fire
- London's Wacky Laws and Traditions
- London's Resident Ravens & Pigeons
- Host a London Trivia Quiz Night

Part X – Make Your Own London Memorabilia

- Create a London Scrapbook
- London Memory Lane Journal
- Design Your Own Coat of Arms
- London Landmark Drawing Challenge
- Make a Postcard About Your Trip
- Plan Your Next London Adventure

Appendix

A. Safety Tips for Young Travelers
B. London-Themed Games
C. Kids Books & Movies Set in London

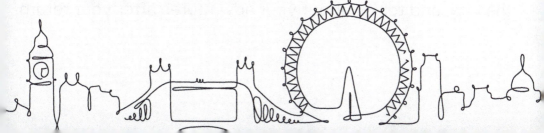

Your London Adventure Starts Here!

London, one of the oldest cities in England, has a rich history stretching all the way back to the Bronze age and the Roman Empire!

Use this guide to learn about some of the most fun and exciting historical places throughout the capital, from iconic landmarks and museums to quirkier attractions and venues showcasing London's vibrant culture and cuisine. You'll soon be navigating London like a local.

How to Use This Travel Guide

This fun travel guide is packed with games, facts, tips and tricks to help you make the most of your trip to London as you explore iconic places in the capital.

The book is divided into ten parts, each covering a different slice of London life and its landmarks. We delve into the fascinating history of the city that became home to the royals and a hub of international trade and innovation as you visit the parks and playgrounds, its haunted palaces and museums where dinosaurs roam.

With this book in hand, write about your expectations before your London visit, record fun facts you find out along the way, and tell us about your adventures after your return.

Before You Arrive in London – Journal Prompts

What are you most excited about seeing or doing in London and why?

___
___
___
___

List eight must-have items you're packing for your trip in the spaces below. Then say why you're taking them.

- ○ ___
- ○ ___
- ○ ___
- ○ ___

- ○ ___
- ○ ___
- ○ ___
- ○ ___

___
___
___

Are you visiting London with family, friends, or on a school trip? Tell us who with and how they'll make your trip fun.

_____
_____
_____
_____
_____

Which places do you want to visit the most and why?

_____
_____
_____
_____
_____

What historical event or figure are you most interested in learning more about while you're in London?

_____
_____
_____
_____
_____

What do you know about the British royal family and what would you do if you met one of them?

_____
_____
_____
_____
_____

What famous London landmarks are you excited to see? Describe why it interests you.

_____

_____

_____

_____

_____

Draw a picture of your favorite London landmark in the box below.

What foods do you want to try while you're in London and how do you think they'll taste?

_____
_____
_____
_____
_____

London is a melting pot of cultures. Which ones are you hoping to learn more about while you're there?

_____
_____
_____
_____
_____

Write about something you hope to experience during your trip to London.

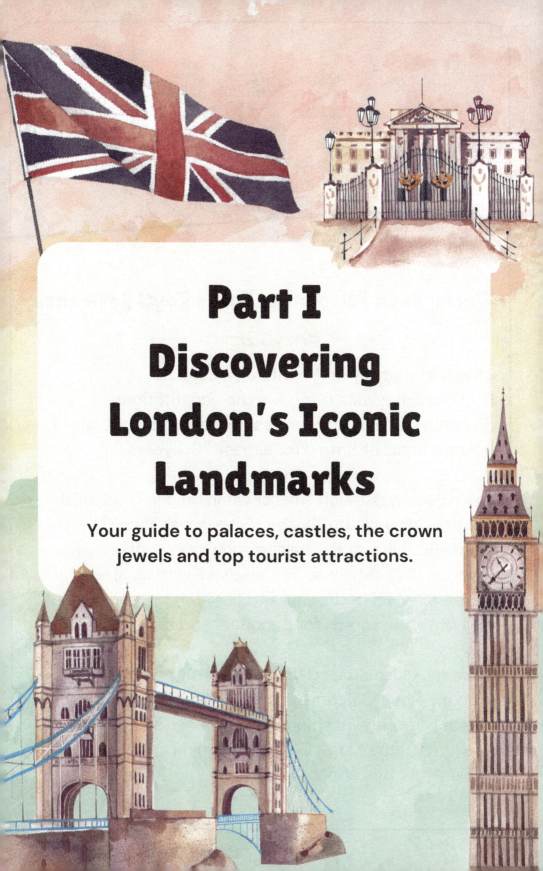

Part I
Discovering London's Iconic Landmarks

Your guide to palaces, castles, the crown jewels and top tourist attractions.

Buckingham Palace: The King's Royal Residence

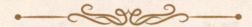

Standing stoically in the City of Westminster, Buckingham Palace has been the constitutional monarch's official London residence in the cultural and political heart of Britain for almost 200 years.

The palace was much smaller when built in 1705 for the Duke of Buckingham. Queen Victoria was the first monarch to live at the palace, moving in with Prince Albert in 1837. She was 'not amused' with its size so she added 52 royal bedrooms and 188 staff bedrooms, plus 19 lavish state rooms for banquets and balls.

Queen Vic also started the trend of making appearances from the Royal Balcony on special occasions. Visit the palace between June and September to see the treasures in the King's Gallery, including Fabergé eggs and artwork by Leonardo da Vinci.

DID YOU KNOW? You can tell a royal guard's regiment by the plume color on his bearskin hat. Grenadier Guards' plumes are white, Coldstream Guards red, Irish Guards blue.

Play 'I Spy the Guard' Game at Buckingham Palace

The King's Guard is made up of many regiments. The sentries standing in their iconic red tunics and bearskin hats are Grenadier Guards.

The guards on horseback are from the Household Cavalry Mounted Regiment known as the King's Life Guard.

Get to the palace gates by 11:00am for the Changing of the Guards led by a marching band on the forecourt every day in the summer and on Mondays, Wednesdays, Fridays and Sundays the rest of the year.

When the sovereign is in residence you'll see the Royal Standard flag flying above the palace and four sentries on duty. When the monarch is not in residence, you'll see only two sentries on duty. Can you spot them all before your friends do?

Meet Beefeaters & Ravens at The Tower of London

The Tower of London is a fortified castle surrounded by a moat overlooking the River Thames, protecting London's rulers and their treasures for more than 900 years, since it was built by William the Conqueror in 1078. As well as officially being His Majesty's Royal Palace, the fortress has served as an armory, a prison, a treasury, home of the Royal Mint, a public record office and a safe place to keep the Crown Jewels of England.

Guarding the tower's treasures are The Yeomen Warders of His Majesty's Royal Palace and Fortress the Tower of London, who are better known as Beefeaters. They also look after the tower's resident ravens, which have lived there since before the reign of King Charles II in the mid 1600s. Legend has it that the tower will collapse and disaster will befall the kingdom if the ravens ever leave the tower.

The Yeoman Warder Ravenmaster looks after the ravens, ensuring they are well fed and housed in cages overnight, releasing them at dawn to roam freely in the castle grounds.

Crown Jewels Treasure Hunt at the Tower of London

There are more than 100 treasures among the Crown Jewels: sacred coronation regalia, orbs, scepters, swords and maces. Can you spot the most precious items in the collection?

St. Edward's Crown

This solid gold crown with a purple velvet cap is a holy relic worn only when crowning a new monarch. The crown has 444 gemstones, including rubies, sapphires, garnets, topazes, and tourmalines.

The Imperial State Crown

The 1937 Imperial State Crown is a copy of the 1838 crown worn by Queen Victoria for her coronation, which was 'squashed like a pudding' when opening Parliament in 1845. Sparkling with 2,868 diamonds, 17 sapphires, 11 emeralds, 269 pearls, and 4 rubies, the crown is worn after coronations and for state events.

The Sovereign's Scepter with Cross

This gold rod in three parts clasping the world's largest cut diamond, the 530.2-carat Star of Africa, represents the sovereign's temporal power and good governance. The scepter with a cross has been used in every coronation since the crowning of Charles II in 1661.

The Sovereign Orb

The gold globe mounted with a cross and encrusted with clusters of emeralds, rubies, sapphires, rose-cut diamonds and pearls represents the sovereign's power and responsibility derived from God. The Orb is placed in the right hand of the monarch during the coronation ceremony.

The Koh-i-Noor

Weighing in at 105.6 carats, the Koh-i-Noor is renowned as one of the world's largest cut diamonds, and is rumored to carry a curse, reportedly bringing death and deprivation to many of the kings, emperors, conquerors and warlords possessing it before it was acquired by Queen Victoria. The diamond is now set in the center of the band of the Crown of Queen Elizabeth the Queen Mother.

The Coronation Spoon

This ornate silver-gilt spoon engraved with acanthus scrolls representing rebirth and immortality has been used by archbishops for centuries to anoint the sovereign with holy oil during coronation ceremonies.

DID YOU KNOW? The Tower of London once had a menagerie of 300 animals, including lions, an elephant and a polar bear.

Seek Out the Secrets of Westminster Abbey

Westminster Abbey is a cavernous treasure trove of ancient artefacts, wall paintings, stained glass windows and tombs with tons of hidden secrets waiting for you to seek out.

This gargantuan Gothic church is literally the seat of power for Britain's reigning monarchs, who are anointed with holy oil and swear a sacred oath while seated in the ancient Coronation Chair, which you can see in St. George's Chapel in the center of the abbey.

The Coronation Chair was made from Baltic oak at least 700 years ago for the coronation of Edward II in 1308.

Thirty kings and queens as well as hundreds of historical celebrities are buried in the abbey's cloisters. Can you find the final resting places of ancient influencers including Charles Darwin, Charles Dickens, Sir Isaac Newton, and Oliver Cromwell?

Look up, too, and marvel at the stained glass windows, including the 300-year old great west window of the nave and the massive south rose window, measuring 100 feet around.

Speak in Secret at St. Paul's Cathedral

The dome and spires of St. Paul's Cathedral sit atop the highest point in London. In fact the dome is one of the highest in the world and the cathedral held the record as the tallest building in London for 253 years.

The cathedral has survived fires, aerial bombings during the World War II Blitz, as well as terrorist attacks and ticking time bombs in its turbulent 300 year history.

But the most fascinating fact about the cathedral is being able to hold secret conversations with someone on the opposite side of the dome's Whispering Gallery.

You'll have to climb a narrow staircase of 259 steps to reach the circular walkway inside the dome, which is adorned with ancient paintings, mosaics and statues.

Use the special acoustic properties of the dome to send your voice around the circular wall to someone on the other side with just a whisper.

 Sir Christopher Wren re-designed St. Paul's cathedral after it was partly destroyed by the Great Fire of London in 1666.

Get an Eyeful of London on the Millennium Wheel

The London Eye, or the Millennium Wheel, is one of the tallest ferris wheels in the world.

Climb into one of the 32 glass pods for a 30-minute ride of a lifetime, taking you to a dizzying height of 443 feet above the River Thames.

On a clear day you can see Windsor Castle, Buckingham Palace and the Olympic Park up to 40 miles away.

Of course, the British weather isn't always on your side, but the ride is thrilling all the same and worth the wait, which can be anywhere between five and 30 minutes or up to an hour on busy days.

DID YOU KNOW? At 400 feet wide, the London Eye is the tallest cantilevered observation wheel in all of Europe.

Take Time Out at the Palace of Westminster

The Houses of Parliament and Elizabeth Tower housing London's most famous bell, Big Ben, are collectively called The Palace of Westminster.

The Houses of Parliament is split into The House of Lords and The House of Commons, which famously survived the Gunpowder Plot hatched by Guy Fawkes to blow up King James I on the 5th of November, 1605.

Big Ben is the largest of the five bells in Elizabeth Tower, chiming on the hour and on special occasions such as New Year's Eve, Christmas Day, and Armistice Day.

You can walk up the 334 steps to the belfry inside the clock tower as part of a 90-minute guided tour.

DID YOU KNOW? The tip of Elizabeth Tower leans north-west by about 500 millimeters (20 inches) due to being built on soft London clay.

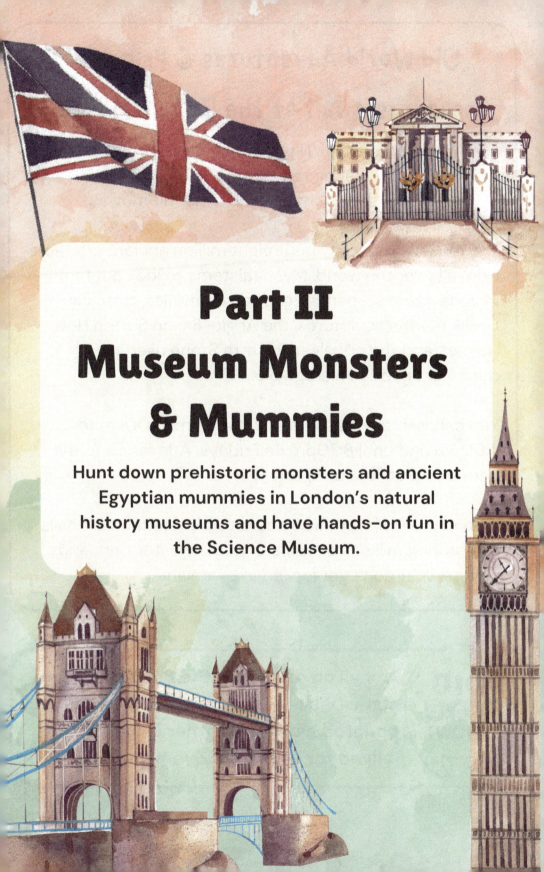

Part II
Museum Monsters & Mummies

Hunt down prehistoric monsters and ancient Egyptian mummies in London's natural history museums and have hands-on fun in the Science Museum.

Old World Adventures & Priceless Treasures Await at the British Museum

If you've seen the film 'Night at the Museum: Secret of the Tomb', you'll recognize the British Museum as the setting for the spooky movie and other hit movies.

The museum houses about eight million ancient artefacts from all over the world. Mystical items to look out for include Aztec serpents, Egyptian mummies, classical Greek marble sculptures, the Anglo-Saxon Sutton Hoo Helmet, and the priceless Rosetta Stone used to decipher Egyptian hieroglyphs.

You can visit the museum any day from 10:00am to 5:00pm and until 8:30pm on Fridays. Admission to the permanent collection is totally free.

Give yourself about three hours to explore the vast halls celebrating millions of years of human history, art, and culture. Just don't get locked in overnight!

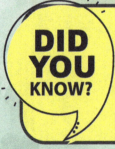

DID YOU KNOW? A snail on display at the British Museum came back to life four years after it was donated along with other snails in 1846. It lived for another six years!

Prehistoric Adventures at the Natural History Museum

Hunt Dinosaurs & Ocean Giants

A trip to the Natural History Museum is an awesome adventure. Explore the natural world of wonders and the history of life on Earth, from the smallest insects to the largest land and marine mammals, plus the dinosaurs that roamed the earth millions of years ago.

In the Dinosaurs gallery, meet Jurassic stars including a roaring Tyrannosaurus Rex, one of the largest carnivores to have stalked the Earth, and the 120-million-year-old Mantellisaurus skeleton – the most complete dinosaur fossil ever found in the UK, plus a triceratops skull, among many other fantastic fossils.

Submerge yourself in the Milstein Family Hall of Ocean Life and be dwarfed by a real skeleton of the largest mammal on earth, the Blue Whale, measuring a massive 25-meters long.

There's so much to learn and much fun to be had exploring collections of meteorites, wildlife, human evolution and space. The museum is open every day except December 24-26 and entry is free.

DID YOU KNOW? The Natural History Museum's Dino Directory lets you explore more than 300 dinosaurs by name, shape or when and where they lived.

Hands-on Fun for Curious Minds at the Science Museum

Are you a budding scientist with a dream to change the world? Have an interactive adventure through time, from the steam age to the space age at the Science Museum, where you can perform fun science experiments and play with tech toys.

In the interactive Wonderlab, you can play with ferrofluid and lightning, make things fizz, pop and glow, and wander around the universe.

In the Volcanoes and Earthquakes gallery you can feel the magnitude of tremors in the earthquake simulator. And in the IMAX cinema you can take a deep sea dive and fly into space in 3D.

Visit any day of the week between 10:00am and 6:00pm. You'll need at least two hours to explore the two levels. Entry is free to see most of the exhibits, except Wonderlab, IMAX and special exhibitions.

Discover the Wonderful World of Art and Design at the V&A Museum

The Victoria & Albert (V&A) museum celebrates art and design, old and new, with over two million objects on display ranging from paintings, sculptures and textiles to costumes, furniture and quirky ornaments.

Here you'll find ceramics, costumes, modern and medieval silver, ironwork, jewelry and more, including Italian Renaissance sculptures and crafts from ancient Asia. Whether you're a budding artist or an antique aficionado, you'll discover a world of curiosities to spark your own creative flare.

The museum is on Cromwell Road in Kensington and open daily from 10:00am until 5:45pm. Entry is free.

Time Travel Through the Streets of London

Take a time-traveling trip through the eyes of Londoners as they tell their stories in an interactive, multimedia biography at the Museum of London.

Venture back to prehistoric times and experience the evolution of Britain's capital through Victorian, Tudor, and Roman times up to modern day. You'll see archeological treasures, photography and fashion, and you'll learn about social and working conditions, protests and women's suffrage that drastically transformed the political landscape.

You'll also hear oral histories from real Londoners and their music as you meander among scale models and relics of the city's suburbs.

If you're a maritime history buff with a thirst for knowledge about the early days of continental trade, the spice wars and how the British became copious tea drinkers, the London Museum Docklands on located in No. 1 Warehouse on the West India Quay of Canary Wharf is well worth a visit. Here you can experience the sight, smells and sounds of Victorian London in the museum's Sailortown, learn about sugar and slavery and the role merchants played when London was at the center of the British Empire and world trade.

Part III
Adventuring in London's Enchanting Parks and Palaces

London's royal green spaces are perfect places to picnic and play with playgrounds abound and abundant wildlife.

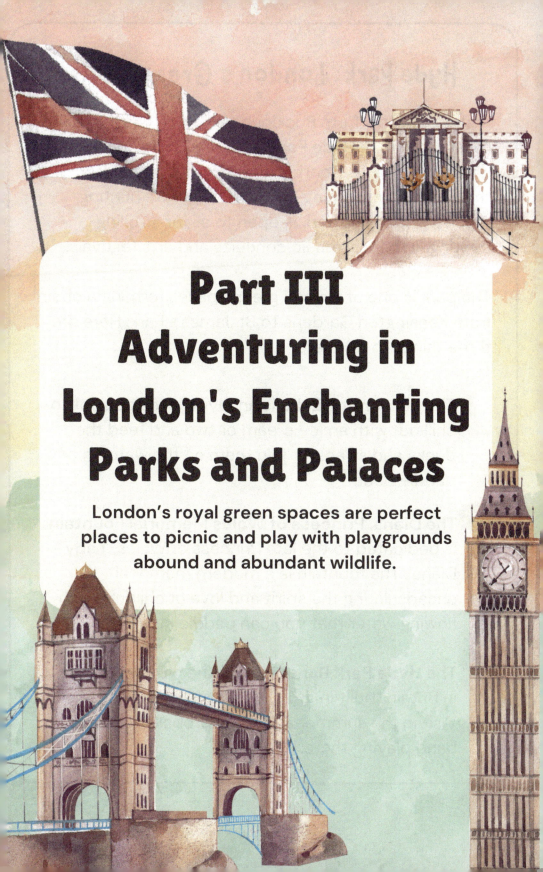

Hyde Park: London's Green Oasis

A stone's throw from Buckingham Palace you'll find the royal gardens of Hyde Park. Covering 350 acres and divided by the Serpentine and the Long Water lakes, the park was once King Henry VIII's private hunting ground. Today the park is open to all for strolling, boating, debating, music concerts and arts festivals.

The park is one of several green spaces forming a chain from Kensington Gardens to St James's Park. Here are three things to do there:

1 **The Serpentine Lake** is an idyllic lakeside spot to chill out with an ice cream or two and feed the ducks and swans, or join them on the water in a paddle boat.

2 **The Diana, Princess of Wales Memorial Fountain** is dedicated to the late Princess of Wales, 'Lady Diana'. The fountain is a modern memorial encapsulating the spirit and love of children with flowing water that you can paddle in.

3 **The Hyde Park Bandstand** is the oldest bandstand in Britain (built in 1869) and is still in use today. Visit in the summer and you'll probably see a live band playing there.

Sometimes, though, there's nothing more pleasant than packing a picnic basket, grabbing a blanket and a ball to hang out on the grass.

For a bit of playtime and the chance to make new friends, pop down to the Hyde Park Playground, where you can climb, swing, and slide to your heart's content.

Have a Splashing Summer at Hyde Park

"Believe me, my young friend, there is nothing – absolutely nothing – half so much worth doing as simply messing about in boats."

– Ratty, *The Wind in the Willows.*

Boating on the Serpentine in summer time is the best way to appreciate the charm of Hyde Park.

From April to October, you can rent a pedalo or row boat for 30 minutes or an hour. Sail around Heron Island and under the Serpentine Bridge under your own power or take it easy in an electric pedalo boat.

Expect to pay £12 and up per adult. Kids aged 3 – 15 are half price. Infants under three years old get to ride for free, under adult supervision of course!

The boating times change as the days shorten in late summer. You can rent the boats between 10:00am and 5:30pm in April and May, until 7:30pm from June to August, then until 6:30pm in September and October.

Pelicans, Playgrounds and Picnics at St. James's Park

This picturesque park behind Buckingham Palace is packed with lakeside adventure and beauty spots. The lush lawns are dotted with playgrounds, picnic tables, and flowerbeds plus it's home to a plethora of wildlife, including a pod of friendly pelicans!

Meet The Pelicans

Pelicans are not native to England so seeing them glide and dive into the water is a strange sight to behold. But they spend a lot of time waddling about on land, too. They're quite friendly, meeting and greeting visitors, and sometimes stopping for a chat on a park bench. Watch them being fed between 2:30pm and 3:00pm each day, next to Duck Island Cottage.

Playgrounds Galore

You'll find some of the best playgrounds in London at St. James's Park, from climbing frames to slides, swings and obstacle courses among the fun outdoor activities to enjoy. Let your imagination run wild as you explore the playgrounds and make a few friends.

Picnic Paradise

St. James's Park is perfect for picnics. Feel free to take your own feast and spread it on the grass or recline in true English summertime style in the deck chairs available for hire from March through to October, or grab a bite and a hot or cold drink at the St. James's Café by the lakeside, or from one of the refreshment kiosks dotted around the park.

Walking & Cycling Trails

Explore the many nature trails and monuments on foot or by pedal power on a self-guided tour of the park. The blooming flowers and blossoms attract all sorts of wildlife in the summertime. You'll also learn lots about historical events and London's heritage at the numerous monuments you can stop at along the way.

Nature Detective in The Regent's Park

Put on your deerstalker hat and keep a sharp lookout as you play Nature Detective, hunting down the abundant wildlife residing at The Regent's Park and Primrose Hill, which is a short tube ride from Hyde Park.

The park is home to more than 120 species of birds and 5,000 varieties of tree. Follow the nature trails around the park and see what you can find in the bushes and trees, as well as Queen Mary's Rose Gardens and the Japanese Garden.

You can even spot more exotic wildlife including lions, monkeys, snakes, tigers and many other interesting creatures at the famous London Zoo, situated in the north corner of The Regent's Park.

Here, little animal lovers can pet goats and other friendly animals at Ambika Paul Children's Zoo. To see the zoo's more ferocious residents, stop by at the Tiger Territory and Land of the Lions enclosure, complete with an Indian-style temple. You can also find an assortment of scaly creatures at the Reptile House.

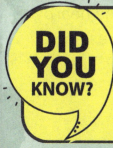

DID YOU KNOW? Kids can splash and climb about on the Gloucester Gate adventure playground behind the London Zoo in The Regent's Park.

Pirate Adventures in Peter Pan's Playground at Kensington Gardens

The gardens of Kensington Palace are a magical place where you can play in the fairytale land of Peter Pan at the The Diana Princess of Wales Memorial Playground.

Climb aboard the huge wooden pirate ship in the middle of the playground, which is just like Captain Hook's ship in Neverland. The playground's ropes and wooden climbing frames are surrounded by sand for soft landings, making the play area safe and exciting for little adventurers. You can camp out in teepees and the wooden forts of the Lost Boy's camp and explore secret tunnels just like Peter Pan's friends in Neverland.

The playground and Diana Memorial area is easily accessible for kids of all ages and abilities, and suitable for wheelchairs, too.

There's a statue of Peter Pan in the park as well, near the Italian Gardens, plus lots of other things to see and do. The gardens are in full bloom in glorious color during the summer with tulips and roses. The Queen Victoria Memorial stands majestically in front of her former residence, Kensington Palace. Inside the nearby Serpentine Gallery see more statues, sculptures and exhibits such as the Suspended States gallery. The gardens are open from 6:00am to 4:30pm.
Entry is free.

A Quick Note for Mom and Dad

Kensington Gardens and Palace have been associated with the magic of Peter Pan for a very long time indeed as the author of this beloved tale, J.M Barrie, lived nearby and was inspired by the gardens to create the timeless tale of the boy who never grew up.

Medieval Adventures & a Maze Challenge in Haunted Hampton Court

Once home to Henry VIII, Hampton Court Palace is a vast Tudor mansion with all kinds of adventures to be had. Explore the great halls and passages inside the palace, which is said to be haunted by the Grey Lady and other spooky spirits.

In the palace grounds, climb atop a dragon and ascend turrets, just like the knights of old in The Magic Garden. Bring some wellies and waterproofs, too, so you can splash about in the fun water features there.

Also take the Hampton Court Maze. challenge and try reaching the middle and back out in under 20 minutes!

Hampton Court Palace & Gardens are open Wednesday to Sunday from 10:00am to 4:00pm. Entry to the gardens is free but there's an admission fee to enter the palace.

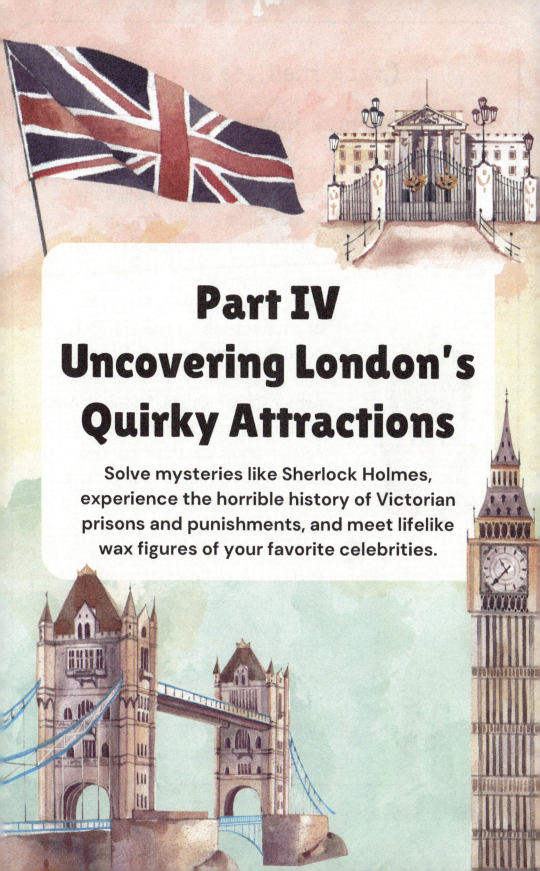

Part IV
Uncovering London's Quirky Attractions

Solve mysteries like Sherlock Holmes, experience the horrible history of Victorian prisons and punishments, and meet lifelike wax figures of your favorite celebrities.

Crack the Case at the Sherlock Holmes Museum

Just off Hampton Court, step inside 221B Baker Street and search for clues to solve mysteries just like the fictional detective Sherlock Holmes and his faithful sidekick, Doctor Watson, in the interactive Sherlock Holmes Museum.

The Georgian townhouse is the original setting for the fictitious adventures of Sherlock Holmes and Dr. Watson, written by author Arthur Conan Doyle. Sherlock was cast as a fan of forensic science, solving crimes with pioneering investigative techniques for the times, residing as a tenant in the townhouse.

Walk through Sherlock's sitting room, laboratory, and study as you look for clues including fingerprints and cryptic messages hidden around the museum to solve a mystery. The museum is open daily from 9:30am to 5:30pm. Entry tickets must be purchased.

Jump Scares & Historical Drama in the London Dungeon

A Scarefest awaits if you're daring enough to step into an interactive world filled with evil characters, torturous contraptions and plague-ridden streets deep inside the London Dungeon.

The scares begin as you descend in a medieval lift and hear horror stories from the real-life dungeon keepers and prisoners that'll send shivers down your spine.

Meet Guy Fawkes in the cellars and experience the horror and stench of the Great Plague as the killer disease swept through the streets of London, leaving blistering bodies in its wake.

In the depths of the dungeon, come face to face with a wicked witch, and test your nerves in the Torture Chamber, or take a stomach-churning drop ride into the abyss.

Find the London Dungeon next to the Millennium Wheel on the East bank of the River Thames. It's open daily from 11:00am to 4:00pm. Tickets must be purchased.

Only the Bravest Survive the Terrors of the London Dungeon

The London Dungeon is so scary that the bone-chilling experience is recommended for kids aged 12 plus with parental guidance. Children under five years old aren't admitted.

If you survive the jump scares and horrors of the London Dungeon, you deserve a badge of honor for your bravery, as this historical attraction is certainly not for the faint hearted.

Do you have what it takes to endure one of the scariest tourist attractions in the city?

Selfies With Stars at Madame Tussauds

Snap a selfie with world-famous celebrities and the royals at London's renowned wax museum Madame Tussauds. The interactive museum near The Regent's Park has eight immersive zones featuring more than 150 incredibly lifelike celebrities, plus plenty of other attractions for a thrilling experience.

The zones feature hyper-realistic wax mannequins of celebrities living and deceased plus iconic comic characters. Meet movie stars, icons of British culture, the cast of Star Wars and practically any famous person you can think of, including notorious villains and murders such as Jack the Ripper. You can also step onto the stage of the Marvel 4D Cinema.

Madame Tussauds is open daily from 10:00am to 3:00pm. Ticket prices vary depending on activities.

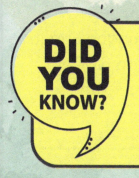

DID YOU KNOW? Madame Tussauds wax figures are made 2% larger than the real person because they melt and shrink over time.

Take an Interactive Tour of London's Oldest and Most Haunted Prison

The Clink Prison Museum is on the site of the oldest prison in London. It's also said to be one of the most haunted places in England. But don't be scared. It's a fun and highly educational experience for all ages.

Take a guided tour or a self-guided tour around the interactive medieval-themed museum filled with real-life characters spinning historical yarns and spooky stories along the way.

The original prison, named Clink Prison because of the sounds of chains being forged by the blacksmith, is nearly 900 years old. The old cells are renowned for numerous ghostly sightings and paranormal activity.

Learn about the history of torture, notorious inmates, and get insights into the evolution of justice and punishment in Britain.

The Clink Prison Museum is located near London Bridge tube station and open daily from 10:00am to 6:00pm. Give yourself an hour and a half to make your way through the attractions.

A Quick Travel Tip

Traveling can be exciting but also tiring! Exploring new places, experiencing new sights, smells, and foods, and meeting new people can take a lot of energy. Don't forget to take some quiet time during your trip, get plenty of rest, and drink lots of water to stay refreshed and ready for more adventures!

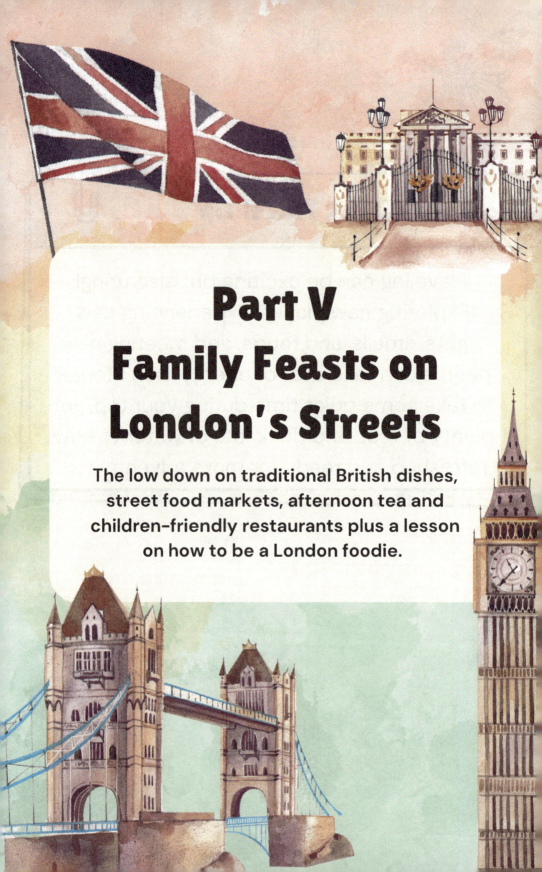

Part V
Family Feasts on London's Streets

The low down on traditional British dishes, street food markets, afternoon tea and children-friendly restaurants plus a lesson on how to be a London foodie.

Traditional British Treats From Fish 'n' Chips to Sherry Trifle

You'll be famished after traipsing round the parks and museums. It's time to taste famous British dishes. Here are some of the dishes you should try while you're in London.

1. Fish 'n' Chips

Nothing fills you up better than a hearty helping of battered fish fillet and chunky chips (fries) served in paper and doused in salt and vinegar. Haddock is considered the best fish to have but pollock and cod are good choices too.

2. Bangers and Mash

Bangers and mash is an absolute classic simple British dish. It's basically juicy sausages served with creamy mashed potatoes topped in rich gravy. The Bangers are traditionally pork or beef Cumberland and Lincolnshire sausages that are seasoned with herbs and spices.

3. Shepherd's Pie

A hot dish served in a deep pan, Shepherd's Pie (also called cottage pie) is traditionally made with minced lamb or beef swimming in gravy and herbs, and topped with a crispy layer of mashed potatoes.

4. Sherry Trifle

Naughty but nice, sherry trifle is a classic fruity dessert traditionally served in English dining rooms after Sunday lunch. Beware, the cream and custard layered on sponge cake soaked in sherry or brandy can make you a little tipsy.

Street Food Feast at Borough Market

Grabbing a bite here is a multicultural experience in the heart of London at the 1,000-year old Borough Market under London Bridge rail pass.

With street vendors offering flavors from around the world alongside great British market favorites , you'll find everything from artisan bakes and organic produce to Thai curries and vegetarian fast food.

Here are three great things to see and do at the market:

1. Samples, Samples, Samples

Kids can be picky eaters but here you can try before you buy with many vendors offering free samples such as cheeses, fruit and freshly baked pastries.

2. The ABC of International Food

See how many foods you can find from different countries. Among the A–Z of regional cuisines are Arabian falafels, French pastries, Italian gelato, Persian curries and spicy Thai. Can you find any starting with Z?

3. Watch Food Being Made

It's impossible to eat everything on sale at the market but watching the street vendors make their food is a rare treat itself. Watch the bakers toss their dough and the chefs put on a fiery show as the smells and sounds engulf you.

Take a Tasting Tour of Borough Market With Drinks & Nibbles

Join gastronomer Celia Brooks to discover the secrets and delights of Borough Market to explore the vast range of exceptional British and international produce there, and learn fascinating facts about the Market's rich history.

Get warmed up and break the ice with a meet and greet session over drinks and pastries at a chic restaurant in the Market before setting off on an exclusive tasting tour.

Celia will show you the best that Borough has to offer and introduce you to bespoke tastings of unique foods and wines. You will taste a bounty of treats, including exceptional charcuterie, many fine cheeses from Britain and beyond, fresh oysters and scallops, hot street snacks, fine chocolate, Sicilian cannoli, plus many more whilst hearing the stories behind the creation of these fabulous artisan foods.

Celia runs public tours on selected Friday mornings from 10:00am to 1:00pm. The tours take about three hours and must be booked in advance via Celia Brooks' website.

Get a Taste of True British Tradition With Afternoon Tea

To truly experience traditional English tastes, take time out to enjoy hot tea and plates piled with sweet treats.

Afternoon tea (high tea) gives you a taste of Great British heritage harking back to the 17th century, when tea was a luxury reserved only for the royals, and those wealthy enough to afford the imported leaves. Here's what you can expect to be served:

- Triangular finger sandwiches with fillings of cream cheese and salmon, fresh cucumber, or egg salad.

- Freshly baked scones served with strawberry jam and clotted cream plus a selection of fruit preserves.

- Teacakes and bakes such as Victoria sponge, Battenberg cake, and Bakewell tarts.

The tea itself is traditionally served in teapot with milk and sugar served separately so you can add them to your preferred taste.

Best Kid-Friendly Restaurants in London

Finding a kid-friendly restaurant that caters to little tummies and palates can be tricky, so here's our pick of the best kid-friendly eateries in central London and dishes they offer for young diners.

1. Coppa Club

With an elevated view of the Tower of London and The Shard, the rooftop restaurant of the Coppa Club has heated glass 'igloos' for alfresco dining in all weathers. It has a varied menu offering plenty of kid-friendly options such as pizza, pasta, burgers, and salads.

2. Hard Rock Cafe Piccadilly Circus

This flagship Hard Rock Cafe in the heart of London serves a fantastic array of American, British, and Canadian dishes with a kid-friendly menu of burgers, fries, pizzas, and milkshakes. The venue is full of rock 'n' roll memorabilia including guitars signed by rock stars, stage props and costumes. Vegetarian, vegan and gluten-free options are also on the menu there.

3. **Inamo Covent Garden**

   The pan-Asian fusion menu at Inamo in Covent Garden offers Japanese, Chinese, Thai and Korean cuisine with a futuristic interactive dining experience to keep kids entertained and in their seats. Order your meals using the touch-screen tables, which have more than 20 video games to play and even let you draw with your fingers.

4. **Where The Pancakes Are London Bridge**

   Only pancakes are on the menu here but the home-made batter and quirky combos of sweet and savory dishes are designed to be nutritious meals that are fun and healthy for all ages. Located between Borough Market and Tate Modern, Where The Pancakes Are serves up pancakes all day long for breakfast, brunch, lunch and dinner with indoor and outdoor seating and lots of activities to keep kids occupied between bites. Watching the pancakes being made is fun too.

5. **Gordon Ramsay Restaurants**

   For a taste of great British grub that the kids will love by celebrity celebrity chef Gordon Ramsey, take the family along to Gordon Ramsay Bar & Grill Mayfair or the Bread Street Kitchen Battersea. As well as classic English dishes such as Beef Wellington and seasonal menus, kids enjoy Gordon's creative takes on burgers, fish and chips and pasta.

Whatever you love to eat, you'll surely find it somewhere in London's many family restaurants specializing in traditional British food and flavors from around the world.

How to Be a London Foodie

Test the abilities of your taste buds as a travelling foodie with our fun Food Critic Challenge. Whether you're dining at a fancy restaurant or grabbing a takeaway, take time to make some notes while you eat so you can rate the dishes and share your opinions with friends. Here's how it works:

1. Before taking your first mouthful, pay attention to how the food is presented and how appetizing or creative it looks.

2. Take a bite and consider how it tastes as well as the texture. Note what you do or don't like about it and whether it reminds you of anything.

3. Devise a rating system for your meals for things like presentation, size and flavor, rating them on a scale of 1 to 5 from terrible to excellent.

4. Write a review your meal by describing the flavors, texture, and how it made you feel.

5. Share your reviews on social media or by simply telling other people about your favorite meals and restaurants.

Have fun filling up and use the Food Critic Challenge as a chance to try something new. You never know, you might fall in love with a new taste sensation!

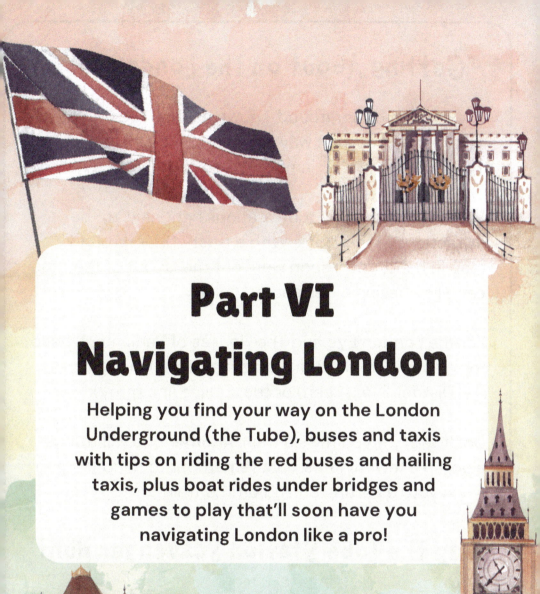

Part VI
Navigating London

Helping you find your way on the London Underground (the Tube), buses and taxis with tips on riding the red buses and hailing taxis, plus boat rides under bridges and games to play that'll soon have you navigating London like a pro!

Getting About on the London Tube

The London Underground, known as 'The Tube', is the quickest and easiest way to get around central London. You avoid the traffic jams and enjoy a fun ride.

You'll find numerous tube stations right next to the attractions in this book. With a trusty Underground map in hand, you'll soon work out the layout of the tube each line having a designated color.

For the London Eye and The Houses of Parliament, head for Westminster Station using the Circle Line (yellow), the District line (green) or the Jubilee line (grey).

Don't worry if you miss a train. Another one will trundle along in a few minutes. Just remember to mind the gap when you're getting on and off the train!

Play the Tube Station Scavenger Hunt

Here's a fun game for all the family as you ride the London Underground. It's like the game 'I Spy' as you try to spot different things at each tube station that you pass through.

The object in question could be a statue, a funny sign, a special color, or something else you're likely to see.

Before you board the train, make a list of things to look for and then see how many you can find as you travel around. It's a great way to make the journey more exciting, and to see some very interesting sights along the way!

Here are some fun things you can add to your list:

- A bird or pigeon
- Someone wearing red trainers
- An old lady pulling a basket trolley behind her
- Someone carrying an umbrella
- A London Underground sign
- A baby in a stroller

You can also add things to your list as you see them and then see how many more you can spot before others as you pull into stations.

Riding London's Iconic Red Buses

A trip on one of London's iconic red double-decker buses is a must while you're in the city.

You can take a sightseeing tour on an open-top double decker or hop on a red Routmaster to get to one of the destinations in this book. Bussing about is a cheap and memorable way to see the sights, especially from the top deck with a bird's-eye view.

Easily plan your bus rides by downloading the TfL Go app to a mobile device. You can't pay for bus fares with cash, so make sure you buy a Visitor Oyster card or have a contactless bank card to tap and pay as you board the front of the bus. Get off using the front or middle doors.

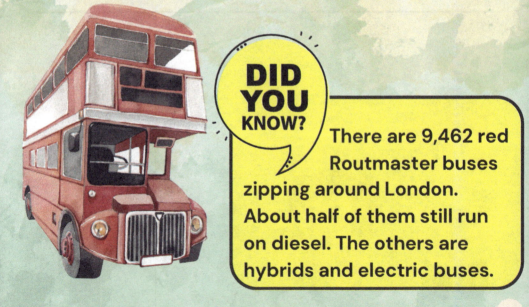

DID YOU KNOW? There are 9,462 red Routmaster buses zipping around London. About half of them still run on diesel. The others are hybrids and electric buses.

Traveling & Tipping in Black Taxis

If you're in a small group, you can hail down one of the famous black taxi cabs seen all over London. They're traditionally called hackney carriages from the days when taxi cabs were horse drawn carriages back in the early 17th century.

Look for vacant cabs with the orange 'TAXI' light on. Up to five people can squeeze into a cab with three on the forward-facing sofa seat, and two more on the folding backward-facing jump seats.

Taxi fares are calculated by the mile. You can pay in cash or with a contactless bank card. It's customary to add a 10 – 15% tip, or at least round off the fare to the nearest pound.

River Thames Boat Rides & Bridges

The winding River Thames divides London in half. At 215 miles long it's the longest river in England, and It's one of the cleanest rivers running through a major city, supporting wildlife and about 125 fish species.

Taking a river cruise is a chilled way to take in the City of London skyline. There are plenty of options available, too, from short half-hour cruises to dinner cruises lasting up to two hours. Most of the boat trips take you past famous landmarks such as The London Eye, The Houses of Parliament, Big Ben and Westminster Abbey.

There are more than 200 bridges crossing the Thames, so why not make it a game to see how many you go under? And can you recognise the most famous of them all, Tower Bridge?

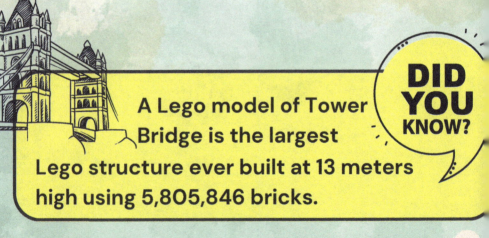

DID YOU KNOW?

A Lego model of Tower Bridge is the largest Lego structure ever built at 13 meters high using 5,805,846 bricks.

Play the London Landmark Bingo Game

If you want to make sure you spot all the must-see sights in London, play London Landmark Bingo while you're riding in a car, a bus or a taxi.

Instead of using numbers like traditional bingo, the aim of this game is to try and spot as many different landmarks as you can during your travels.

Prepare your bingo card by downloading images of the top ten London landmarks and sticking them on it. When you see one of the landmarks, cross it out on your card until you have a row or a full house. Here's our recommendation for the top ten London landmarks to put on your bingo card.

- Big Ben (also known as the Elizabeth Tower)
- Tower Bridge
- Buckingham Palace
- The London Eye
- St. Paul's Cathedral
- The Shard
- Trafalgar Square
- The Houses of Parliament
- Covent Garden
- Piccadilly Circus

Add more if you like but it's best to make it an even number.

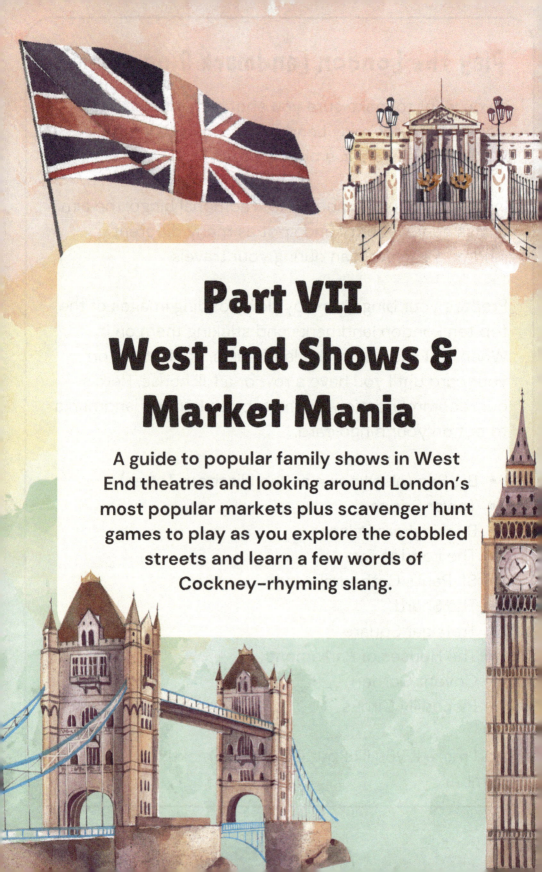

Part VII
West End Shows & Market Mania

A guide to popular family shows in West End theatres and looking around London's most popular markets plus scavenger hunt games to play as you explore the cobbled streets and learn a few words of Cockney-rhyming slang.

Dazzling Entertainment Awaits in the West End's Theatreland

London's West End is the glitzy side of the city with dozens of theatres showing popular musicals, hit plays and new stage productions. Here in 'Theatreland' you'll find shows for all ages and tastes, from classic musicals such as *The Phantom of The Opera* and *Les Miserables* to contemporary productions for younger audiences, including *The Lion King*, *Matilda* and *Harry Potter and the Cursed Child*.

You'll find the main theatres along Shaftesbury Avenue, which is home to the famous venues such as the Apollo Theatre, Palace Theatre, Old Vic and many more.

To reach the West End on the tube, head for Piccadilly Circus, Leicester Square or Tottenham Court Road on the Piccadilly and Bakerloo lines.

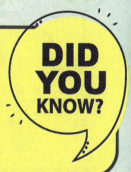

Harry Potter fans can actually stand in front of Platform 9 ¾ at King's Cross Station, where Harry boards the Hogwarts Express.

Put On Your Own West End Show

Are you a budding thespian inspired by the dazzle of West End shows?

If you enjoyed the theatrics on London's stages, why not get together with your friends and act out your favorite scenes?

Find some props and costumes to dress the part and let your imaginations do the rest. After a few rehearsals, put on a performance for family and friends.

Who knows, maybe this will be your big break? And next it'll be your name in flashing lights above the theatre doors!

DID YOU KNOW? Just off the West End is a book lover's paradise with antiquarian book shops galore along Charing Cross Road.

Quirkiness & Circus Acts at Covent Garden

Wandering along the cobbled streets of Covent Garden lined with craft stores, boutiques and cafes, has a distinctly Dikensian feel and resembles scenes from Diagon Alley in the Harry Potter series.

Here in the heart of the West End, street performers entertain shoppers with music, magic and daring circus acts. In the nooks and crannies of this open-air market you'll find antiques, trinkets, crafts, clothes and lots of fantastic food.

The neighborhood's charming Victorian streets are divided into three parts. Find arts and crafts, wellness products and more in the shops along Seven Dials and Neal's Yard, or shop among the stalls in the bustling Market Building and Piazza.

To get there on the Underground, take the Piccadilly Line to Covent Garden Station or at peak times, get off at Leicester Square.

Have a Luvly Jubbly Day Out at London's Markets

Markets abound in central London offer a plethora of places to immerse yourself in the local culture. Explore the alternative fashion scene in Camden Market or hunt for antiques and other vintage wares at Portobello Market, plus much more besides.

Here's our pick of the popular markets you can easily visit and the kinds of stalls you can find:

1. **Borough Market**

    London's oldest street food market.

2. **Old Spitalfields Market**

    Quirky crafts, art, and funky fashion.

3. **Columbia Road Flower Market**

    Pick up a bouquet from the stunning flower stalls.

4. **Brick Lane Market**

    Flea market with second-hand goods and bric-a-brac.

5. **Covent Garden Market**

    Fruits and vegetables, art, jewelry, cafes and more.

6. **Greenwich Market**

    Food, antiques, arts and crafts.

These are just a few of the most popular markets in central London but there are many more dotted around the city, offering a fun opportunity to immerse yourself in London's culture and meet some of the locals.

Market Mania Scavenger Hunt

For an extra dose of fun when you visit one of the London markets, why not try the Market Mania Scavenger Hunt?

Make a list of items and oddities to find or challenges to complete, such as trying a new food, finding a particular piece of clothing or taking a selfie with a street Performer.

Then set off on your scavenger hunt adventure with your family and see who can complete the most tasks. It's a great way to explore these markets, interact with a few locals, and make some fun memories together.

DID YOU KNOW? The oldest and one of the largest toy stores in the whole world is Hamleys on Regent Street. It's stocked with more than 50,000 lines of toys on seven floors!

Speak Slang Like a Local Londoner

Finally, and most importantly, to truly immerse yourself in London's traditional culture, try talking to the locals in their own unique dialect – Cockney rhyming slang.

You probably already know some phrases such as 'cheers, mate' (thank you) or 'blimey' (wow) but there are hundreds of words and phrases that can leave you scratching your head if you've never heard them before. Here are ten Cockney phrases you might hear:

"You're telling porkies" – You're telling lies.
"You wouldn't Adam an' Eve it!" – You wouldn't believe it!
"Sounds a bit dodgy to me" – Sounds suspicious.
"Let's 'ave a butchers" – Let me have a look.
"I'm on me jack jones" – I'm on my own.
"I need a jimmy riddle" – I need to take a pee.
"I seen it with me own mince pies" – I saw it with my own eyes.
"Bob's your uncle" – There you have it, simple.
"Proper job" – Good job, excellent.
"Get him on the dog 'n' bone" – Call him on the phone.

Walking and talking Cockney might be 'knackering' but the locals will be 'chuffed to bits' if you can keep up with their lingo.

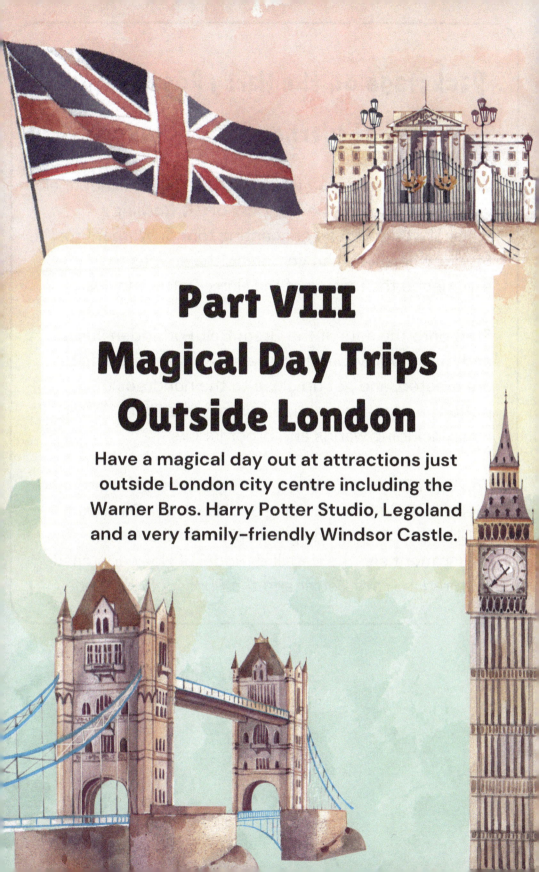

Part VIII
Magical Day Trips Outside London

Have a magical day out at attractions just outside London city centre including the Warner Bros. Harry Potter Studio, Legoland and a very family-friendly Windsor Castle.

Backstage on the Harry Potter Movie Set at Warner Bros. Studio

Walk in the footsteps of Britain's most famous fictional wizard and explore the wonders of J.K. Rowling's magical world with an enchanting tour of Warner Bros. Studio, where you can go behind the scenes to experience the making of the Harry Potter movies.

Step onto the sets of the Great Hall, Forbidden Forest and Diagon Alley. See how the magical special effects are created, and get up close to the hundreds of potions and other props featured in the Harry Potter films, including wands and broomsticks.

You can also meet the magical creatures that Harry and friends encounter, including Buckbeak, the Basilisk, goblins and Aragog the giant spider. In the Art Department see the detailed model of Hogwarts castle featured in *Harry Potter and the Philosopher's Stone*.

Make a Hit Movie Like Harry Potter

Parents and teachers can access virtual learning materials for use at home or in the classroom from The Making of Harry Potter website, where you can download up to 12 week's worth of activity worksheets.

The activity worksheets offer fun learning experiences and inspiration for a career in creative industries with each activity focused on a specific aspect of the filmmaking process and business.

Using the sheets, you'll learn all the steps it takes to make a hit movie from scratch. You'll learn how to come up with storylines, costumes and characters so you can pitch your idea to the major studios.

When it comes to making a movie, you'll need to know about camera angles, set design, make up and much more, as well as the business side of making a box office blockbuster.

A Royal Day Out at Windsor Castle

Set in glorious grounds about 25 miles outside the city center, Windsor Castle is the oldest and largest occupied castle in the world. Visiting is fun and educational with family activities and guided tours specially for children aged 7 to 11.

Wandering around the opulent state rooms adorned with portraits and chandeliers gives you a rare glimpse into the luxurious lives of the British Royals, past and present. Can you find Queen Mary's doll's house among the treasures on display?

The Pug Yard Learning Centre offers special activities in school holidays, or you and your family can take a free multimedia tour around the castle with Scorch the dragon. See the Changing of the Guard here too.

DID YOU KNOW? The City of London is guarded by dragons! Keep your eyes peeled for dragon statues protecting the city entrances.

Building Adventures for All Ages at Legoland Windsor Resort

Have a fun-filled family day out at Legoland Windsor Resort theme park, where Lego creations come to life and you can have the ride of your life with more than 55 interactive attractions for all ages.

Walk around wet and dry themed lands, and get a bird's-eye view over a scale model of London made entirely out of Lego bricks.

Watch shows, ride the dragon roller coaster, and even create your own Ferrari race car and test drive it at the LEGO Driving School. Younger drivers can enjoy the Lego DUPLO build zone, where they can splash about and design their own Ferrari with bigger bricks.

Become a Master Builder at Legoland

If you're a budding builder or just love Lego, the Master Builder game at Legoland Windsor is a must-try.

You will be given a set of fun challenges to complete throughout the entire park, such building the tallest Lego tower or creating a Lego masterpiece based on a particular theme.

Be sure to have your thinking cap on and let your creativity soar while you work with others to solve puzzles and construct your creations.

The Master Builder game encourages teamwork, problem solving, and hands-on learning, making it a fun and educational experience for the whole family.

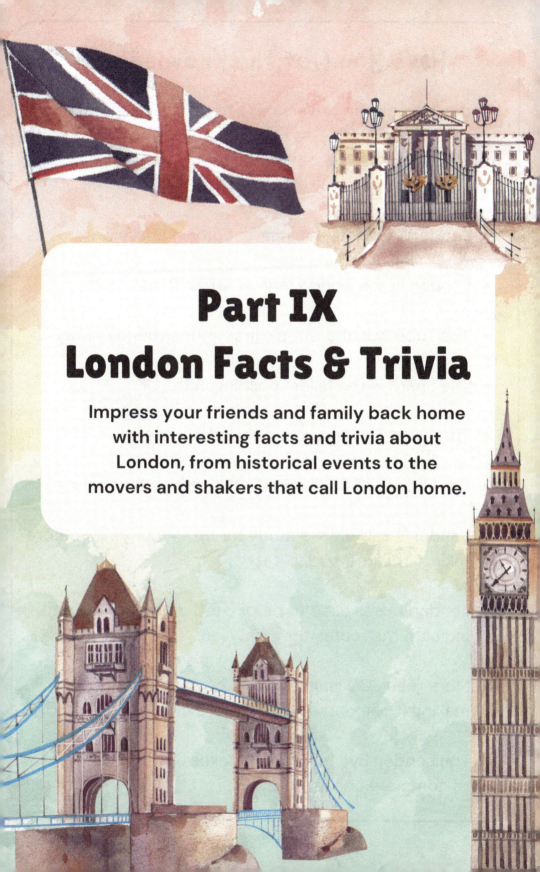

Part IX
London Facts & Trivia

Impress your friends and family back home with interesting facts and trivia about London, from historical events to the movers and shakers that call London home.

Have You Got the Knowledge?

London's black cab drivers have to pass a tough test called 'The Knowledge' to prove that they know all the routes by heart. Here are 10 fun facts to memorize so you can show off your knowledge about London.

- London Proper is the smallest city in England.

- London is the world's largest urban forest.

- The Tube was the world's first underground railway.

- The Shard is the tallest building in the UK.

- The Great Fire wiped out a third of the city.

- The Houses of Parliament is the UK's largest palace.

- London's cab drivers study for up to four years before taking 'The Knowledge' test.

- London buses used to be painted different colors to indicate the routes they traveled.

- More than 300 languages are spoken in London, making it one of the most diverse cities in the world.

- The London Eye ferris wheel takes about 30 minutes to complete one full rotation.

Famous Londoners Who Shaped British Culture & History

Apart from the royals that call London their home, many of the world's influencers and celebrities, living and departed, hail from the streets of London.

Literary Giants
As the setting for the adventures of Oliver Twist, Charles Dickens used the 19th-century poor houses, prisons and markets of London, as did Samuel Pepys in his daily diary entries.

Silver Screen Actors
Award-winning cockney actor Michael Caine grew up in Southwark, South London and starred in 160 films over an 80-year career. Charlie Chaplin also grew up in South London, enduring childhood poverty in work houses without a father, while his mother committed to an asylum when he was 14 years old.

Musicians & Singers
London has produced many world-class entertainers from rock legends David Bowie and Mick Jagger (Rolling Stones) to Paul McCartney (The Beatles) and Amy Winehouse.

A New London Rises From the Ashes After the Great Fire

The Great Fire of London in 1666 is said to have started at a bakery in Pudding Lane. The fire blazed for four days, razing thousands of homes and businesses across about a third of the city; an area equivalent to 280 football pitches.

The fire spread quickly, as most of the buildings were made of wood, destroying 13,000 houses and 87 churches, leaving 100,000 people homeless.

However there was a silver lining to the tragedy. The fire brought a swift end to the plague that had ravaged the city and killed about one fifth of the population by wiping out the diseased rats and their fleas responsible for the outbreak.

A new, improved London with better buildings and infrastructure, rose from the ashes.

Wacky London Laws & Traditions

Did you know that it's illegal to die in the Houses of Parliament, or that it's against the law to handle a salmon suspiciously in public?

These are some of the many laws written hundreds of years ago that seem completely wacky in modern days. For example, it's also against the law to shake your rug in the street, and it wasn't until 1976 that a law was repealed requiring London taxi drivers to carry a bale of hay for their horses.

While gambling is legal in London, you can't do it in a library, and you're not allowed to have a pig sty in front of your house, or walk cows through the streets during the daytime.

As for quirky traditions, the Peter Pan Cup is a swimming race held in Hyde Park on Christmas Day with hardy participants swimming a 100-yard stretch of the freezing Serpentine.

And every September a herd of sheep is driven across London Bridge in a tradition started by the Worshipful Company of Woolmen in 1180 to check the quality of wool coming into London.

London's Resident Ravens & Pigeons

Ravens have lived at the Tower of London for hundreds of years. Legend says the kingdom will fall if they leave.

Charles II decreed that at least six ravens must always be in residence at the tower. As a result, the ravens' wings are traditionally clipped. The six ravens residing at the tower today are named Jubilee, Harris, Poppy, Georgie, Edgar, and Branwen.

Thousands of pigeons used to hang around in Trafalgar Square, perching on the heads and arms of visitors feeding them. But the Mayor of London banned feeding pigeons in the area in 2003 and introduced hawks to keep the pigeons away. Now only a few hundred pigeons occupy the area.

DID YOU KNOW? King Charles II initially ordered the ravens to be removed from the Tower of London but changed his mind after a string of bad luck.

Host a London Trivia Quiz Night

With all the facts and figures you've learned from this book and from the places you visited on your trip to London, why not test your friends and family on what they can recall from their visit to see who'll be the reigning London Trivia Champion?

As the quizmaster, prepare questions and answers on cards or pieces of paper from your notes, before gathering your friends or family around for a quiz night. Make sure the players can't see the answers!

Participants can pull random questions from a hat or you can have them spin a wheel or roll a dice to get a question based on one of these six topics: Landmarks; The Royal Family; Quirky Laws; Food & Drink; The Crown Jewels; London Transport.

Create several questions for each topic. For example, under the topic Royal Family, ask questions such as, 'Who was the first queen to live at Buckingham Palace?' (Queen Victoria), and 'How many Kings have been named Charles?' (three). For the Landmarks topic, ask questions such as, 'What is another name for the London Eye?' (see page 16) and for Transport, you could ask, 'How many passengers can fit in a London taxi?' (can you remember?).

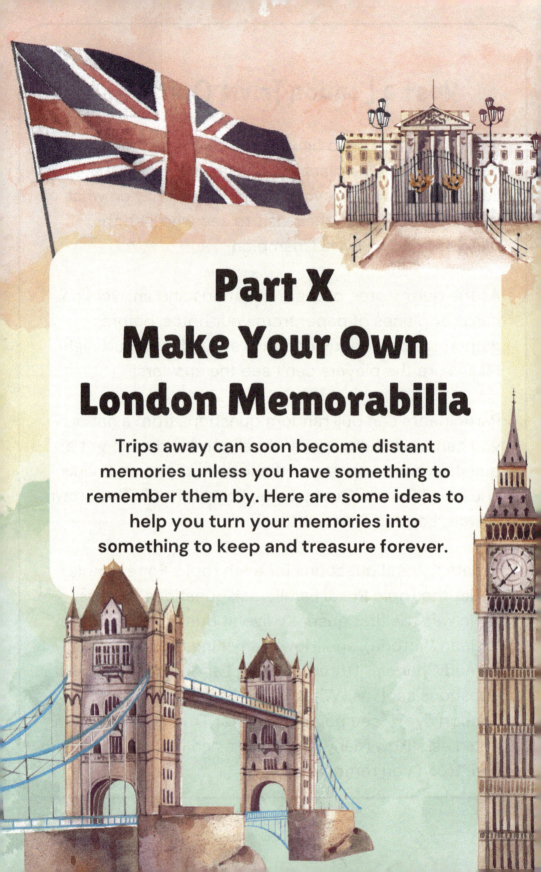

Part X
Make Your Own London Memorabilia

Trips away can soon become distant memories unless you have something to remember them by. Here are some ideas to help you turn your memories into something to keep and treasure forever.

Create a London Scrapbook

Creating a London scrapbook is a fun and creative way to document your adventures in the city!

Start by collecting souvenirs such as ticket stubs, postcards and brochures from the places you visit to cut and stick on your scrapbook pages.

Then decorate each page and add captions or notes about your experiences.

Anything goes! You can include photos of iconic landmarks, sketches of street scenes, and even pressed leaves or flowers that you found along the way.

In years to come, your London scrapbook will become a treasured keepsake filled with memories of your time exploring this vibrant city that you can show off to your friends and family.

London Memory Lane Journal

Keeping a journal or diary as you explore London helps you remember all the details about your visit. Use the journaling prompts at the top of the next few pages to write diary entries in the space below.

What were your first thoughts when you arrived in London, and what did you see, hear and smell?

_____
_____
_____
_____
_____
_____
_____
_____

Tell a story about something funny or unexpected that happened to you in London.

Write about seeing a famous landmark such as Buckingham Palace or the Tower of London. What did you learn and what was your favorite part?

Talk about London's rich history by describing something interesting you learned about the city's past.

If you visited a museum, write about an exhibit you liked and why it fascinated you.

If you visited one of London's many parks, write about it here and describe a fun activity that you did there.

_____
_____
_____
_____
_____
_____
_____
_____
_____
_____
_____
_____
_____
_____
_____

Tell us about the most interesting food you tried in London and how it tasted.

How did you get around the city? Write about your experience riding taxis, the iconic red buses or the Underground.

Write about the most interesting person you met in London and your interaction with them.

Describe a busy street or market you visited. What were the sights, sounds, and smells?

Describe your favorite moment in London and why it was special.

Design Your Own Coat of Arms

Design your very own family coat of arms, just like those seen at royal places and on important buildings around the City of London.

A coat of arms describes your family's origins, occupation and values in pictures and colors. It usually includes a shield, a helmet and a motto. Sometimes a crest is added on top of the helmet and supporters on each side, which are often animals.

The Shield
This is the centerpiece of your coat of arms representing two sides of a family (your lineage), one side for mom and one side for dad. Use colored symbols to represent something about each of your parent's origins.

The Helmet
The helmet goes above the shield to represent something that defines you. Royals have a crown here but you could use something to represent a sport, a hobby or a career that you're passionate about.

The Motto
Think of a few words to describe your values or what kind of person you are and write them on a ribbon underneath the shield.

London Landmark Drawing Challenge

Put your artistic skills to the test with the London Landmark drawing challenge!

Choose a famous London landmark such as Tower Bridge or Buckingham Palace and challenge yourself to draw it from memory. Pay attention to details such as architectural features, proportions, and perspective as you sketch your chosen landmark.

You can use pencils, markers, or digital drawing tools such as PhotoShop to create your masterpiece. Don't worry about making it perfect. Just have fun and express your creativity!

Share your drawings with friends and family or display them in your home as a reminder of your trip to London.

Make a Postcard About Your Trip

Make your own postcard about your London getaway and post it to someone special

First get a blank A6 sized piece of card or cut a rectangle that's 7 inches long and 5 inches wide. Lie the card horizontally for a landscape design.

Choose a side to draw a picture of something you did or saw in London, or print out a photo to stick on the card instead. On the other side draw a vertical line down the middle of the card. On the left side write a short message to the recipient. On the right side write the recipient's name and address. Leave enough space in the top right corner to add a stamp.

Now head off to a local post office to buy a stamp and send your postcard by snail mail. Your recipient will be delighted to hear from you!

Plan Your Next London Adventure

Get ready for your next London adventure by planning ahead and making a list of all the things you want to see and do that you missed last time or just can't wait to do again!

Start by researching attractions, events, and activities that interest you, from world-class museums to hidden gem neighborhoods. Check the dates and opening times that you'll be able to go.

Create a detailed itinerary of the places you want to visit along with times and dates for each activity. Remember to include travel times and leave time for spontaneous discoveries along the way.

Next you can start making reservations by phone or online for tours, shows, and dining experiences to ensure you don't miss out on anything. Make sure you get permission from Mom or Dad first, and ask for their help arranging things!

With careful planning and preparation, your next London adventure is sure to be an unforgettable experience!

Appendix

We've almost made it to the end of our book. In this short, final section, you'll find some fun ideas for games and activities to pass the time during your travels plus ways to make your trip fun and educational. Most importantly, read the tips on staying safe and asking for help.

Safety Tips for Young Travelers

Before going to London, prepare a card to carry in your pocket or bag with an adult's contact details in case you get separated. Don't be afraid to ask for help from police officers and trustworthy people.

Below are a few useful phrases to practice saying in case you need any help:

1. **"Excuse me, where is the nearest toilet?"**
   Say this when you need the bathroom but don't know where it is.

2. **"Can I have a ticket, please?"**
   Use this when buying tickets for public transportation or attractions.

3. **"How much does it cost?"**
   Helpful for finding out prices for things like food, souvenirs, or activities.

4. **"Please" and "Thank you"**
   Always remember your Ps and Qs to be polite when interacting with others.

5. **"I'm lost. Can you help me find my parents?"**
   Important to know in case you get separated from your family in a crowded place.

London-Themed Games

Don't let the fun stop as your London trip comes to an end. Here are a few fun games you can play on your journey home:

1. **London Landmark Bingo**

   Make a bingo card with famous London landmarks and see who can spot them first on the journey home. See page 56 for instructions.

2. **I Spy London Edition**

   Take turns describing things you see out the window using clues such as colors, shapes, or the letters the words begin with.

3. **London Trivia Quiz**

   Test each other's knowledge of London with questions about landmarks, history, and culture.

4. **Create Your Own Silly London Story**

   Tell a story starting with "I went to London and I.... ", adding something you did or saw. Then each person in your group takes a turn adding another sentence to the story. It can be something totally made up. Make it as silly as you like!

5. **Draw Your Favorite London Memory**

   Grab a piece of paper and draw or paint a memory of your favorite moment from your trip to London.

Kids Books & Movies Set in London

Here are some classic must reads and movies to check out before you visit London to get a feel for why the city is so special or to relive memorable moments from your trip:

Books

- **Paddington Bear** by Michael Bond. A series of illustrated books following the adventures of a lovable refugee bear from Peru as he explores London.

- **The London Eye Mystery** by Siobhan Dowd. Join siblings Ted and Kat as they solve a mysterious disappearance during a ride on the Millennium Wheel.

- **This is London** by M. Sasek. Explore the sights and sounds of London through colorful illustrations and fun facts.

- **Peter Pan** by J.M. Barrie. Journey to Neverland with Peter, Wendy, and the Lost Boys in this classic tale set in Victorian London.

- **Mary Poppins** by P.L. Travers. Meet the magical nanny who takes the Banks children on fantastical adventures through London.

Movies

- **Harry Potter.** Follow young wizards Harry, Hermione, and Ron in a series of eight fantastical films as they attend Hogwarts School of Witchcraft and Wizardry and explore a magical side of London.

- **Peter Rabbit.** Join Peter Rabbit and his animal friends as they embark on mischievous adventures in London and the English countryside.

- **101 Dalmatians.** Follow the adventures of pet dogs Pongo and Perdita as they rescue their puppies from the clutches of the villainous Cruella de Ville in London.

- **Oliver Twist.** Experience the classic tale by Charles Dickens about an orphaned boy navigating the streets of Victorian London in search of a home and family.

- **The Parent Trap.** Follow twins Annie and Hallie as they hatch a plot to reunite their long-lost parents during a summer vacation in London.

Thank you for taking the time to read my book!

I hope it has enhanced your time in London and added to your adventure. If you enjoyed my guide, I would truly appreciate it if you could take a moment to leave a review. Your feedback not only helps other travelers but also inspires me to continue creating helpful resources. I read every review and value your thoughts!

Jessica Woodson xx

Made in United States
North Haven, CT
30 June 2025

70213242R00059